THE SEXUAL REVOLUTION

Also by Jack Dominian

CHRISTIAN MARRIAGE
MARITAL BREAKDOWN

The Church and the Sexual Revolution

JACK DOMINIAN

DARTON, LONGMAN & TODD
LONDON

First published in Great Britain in 1971
by Darton, Longman & Todd Limited
85 Gloucester Road, London SW7
© 1971 by J. Dominian
All biblical quotations are from The Jerusalem Bible
© 1966 by Darton, Longman & Todd Ltd and
Doubleday & Co Inc.
Made and printed in Great Britain by
Northumberland Press Limited
Gateshead
ISBN 0 232 51152 7

CONTENTS

	INTRODUCTION	7
I	*The Church and the Sexual Revolution*	9
II	*The Nature of Sexuality*	17
III	*Growing Towards Marriage*	24
IV	*Sexuality in Marriage*	33
V	*Children*	42
VI	*Sexual Deviations*	50
VII	*The Single State*	59
VIII	*The Power of Positive Love*	67
	NOTES	74

INTRODUCTION

This book contains eight essays on human sexuality, seven of which appeared in *The Tablet* during the latter months of 1970. The eighth – though it occurs as the fifth in the collection – was written specially for this publication. The subjects of the essays had as their underlying theme the confrontation of sexual attitudes today with Christianity, the Roman Catholic community being particularly in mind.

Traditional views have been examined afresh in the light of new knowledge and different perspectives; especial attention has been paid to those insights derived from psychology and psychiatry which have made a revolutionary impact on our understanding of human nature. As far as possible, controversial issues have been described fairly. However, in the author's opinion, far too much attention is given to these topics by people in general who lack the informed background that is essential if an objective evaluation is to be made. Christianity has a unique responsibility to make a careful judgement concerning what is truly consistent with human dignity in the changes occurring amid our society. Labelling such changes indiscriminately and negatively as innovations of the 'permissive society' is a facile way out for the escapist. For hundreds of years, Christianity has done less than justice to one of the creator's most enriching dimensions of the human personality, and today – now – it can at last make amends.

What is needed, then, is an informed Christian community, ready to examine without prejudice the advances made by the behavioural sciences, assessing their discoveries in an unceasing dialogue with the truths of revelation. This approach will ensure that whatever enhances man's stature will be accepted, and whatever is inimical to human love rejected. In a pluralistic society such as ours the role of the Christian is more vital than ever, not as a hostile judge but as a caring, compassionate and discerning contributor affirming all that is human, truly reflecting the image of God in man.

With this in mind, the essays were written. Much had to be left unsaid that I hope will nevertheless emerge in the reflections and discussions that they may provoke.

My sincere thanks are due to the editor of *The Tablet*, Mr T. Burns, and to my publishers for their encouragement and support.

J. DOMINIAN
Rickmansworth, January 1971

I

The Church and the Sexual Revolution

MANY MEN AND women, of all faiths or of none at all, have suffered intense distress and dismay over the contemporary approach to sexuality in our society. However, others – Christian, non-Christian, and those who believe that they care for human values to an equal degree of sensitivity – have at the same time rejected such perturbation as petulant and anachronistic.

Throughout this century, millions of words and many acrimonious exchanges have passed between people of undoubted honesty and integrity who have adopted diametrically opposing views, and who accuse each other with utter sincerity of betraying human values. Words like 'love', 'affection', 'sexuality', 'corruption', and 'obscenity' are used very frequently to portray man's deepest yearnings and fears, and yet it is possible to reach totally divergent conclusions about the meaning and significance of each one of these terms.

These chapters have therefore been written in an attempt to elucidate as far as possible, in the light of contemporary knowledge and attitudes, the issues which evoke such contrasting feelings. For a few this examination will itself appear to be provocative, and some of the opinions expressed unacceptable. Such extremely serious conflict and tension in this and other areas among Christians can be justified by one — and only one — reason: namely, a *prima facie* case that large numbers of truly sincere Christians feel that they are unable to do justice to the image of God in their humanity within the tenets of the Christian conception of the nature of man. This is certainly the case in the field of sexuality and marriage, and Christians of all denominations have subscribed to this view.

Professor Noonan's book, *Contraception*,[1] indirectly documents the views of Catholics; Dr J. A. T. Robinson is well known for his uncompromising stand;[2] the British Council of Churches issued a report, *Sex and Morality*, in 1966;[3] the Quakers offered in 1963 their contribution, *Towards a Quaker View of Sex*; from the United States Joseph Fletcher's book *Situation Ethics*[4] is considered a controversial landmark and a more recent book, *Honest Sex*,[5] summarises similar points of view. Books opposing and protesting against this trend include *The New Morality*[6] and Leslie Paul's *Coming to Terms with Sex*.[7]

These prominent works, amongst many others, indicate clearly that this is an area of human concern which demands attention. It can no longer be buried or dismissed as of secondary importance by those who consider that too much attention is being paid to this topic. It hardly needs to be said that the twentieth century did not discover sexuality. After all, sexuality has confronted man since the beginning of time. What is undoubtedly new is the evolution of human consciousness to a point where in large areas of the Western world, men and women have become free from the pressing anxieties of material survival and are now able to realise more fully a deeper layer of their human potential in which feelings, emotions and instincts play a significant part in living.

For the Christian, however, no evolution of human behaviour is acceptable which is not in harmony with the prescribed ideals in the Scriptures. And here of course many difficulties exist. The Old Testament and the New consist of a multiplicity of texts and positive directions. Contemporary exegesis of all denominations warns against the selective quotation of single texts and emphasises the need to see patterns. This is absolutely true in the case of sexuality, in which there is a readily available quote to prove anything, particularly if the case that has to be made is negative. A much more complex situation is now in evidence in which man's growing awareness of himself needs determining and shaping in an evolving dialogue with the Scriptures. Nevertheless, certain features are consistently present and must form the essential background for any discussion.

The Old Testament

Verse 31 of the first chapter of Genesis states categorically: 'God saw all he had made, and indeed it was very good.' This sentence gives us confidence to examine every aspect of human behaviour in terms proclaiming its intrinsic and potential goodness. And this clearly applies to all that is collectively designated as sexual.

Having indicated that God found all that he had made very good, the second chapter of Genesis immediately pin points the first fundamental factor. Human sexuality demands a *relationship*, its characteristic feature *is* its relational character. 'It is not good that the man should be alone.'

Anthropologists have shown the wide variety of combinations of heterosexual relationships which can be called marriage. Israel, despite being surrounded by tribes which practised polygamy and worshipped gods associated with fertility, chose monogamy and monotheism, worshipping Yahweh, a celibate God. The personal characteristics which were to be explored in marriage are portrayed by the prophet Hosea, who compares the relation between husband and wife with that between Yahweh and His people and uses such language as: 'I will betroth you to myself for ever, betroth you with integrity and justice, with tenderness and love.'[8]

The ability to give expression to these personal characteristics is of course restricted by the social exigencies of the period, of which the crucial one was the inequality of the sexes. The Decalogue includes a man's wife among his possessions along with his house and land, his male and female slaves, his ox and his ass.[9] The glory of the wife, and her undoubted purpose, was to bear children. Children are the 'crown of man' and the procreational aspect of sexuality stands supreme in the Old Testament.

But the erotic, the joy of physical beauty and its pleasure are fully acknowledged. There is no condemnation of sexual pleasure as such in the Old Testament; on the contrary, it is portrayed vividly. Much has been written about the theology of the Song of Songs but it is now accepted as the celebration of the fidelity and love between man and woman in a collection of love poems. For those distrustful of the erotic the language of the Canticle of Canticles must be surprising to say the least, if not shocking.

How beautiful are your feet in their sandals,
O prince's daughter!

> The curve of your thighs is like the curve of a necklace,
> work of a master hand.
>
> Your navel is a bowl well rounded
> with no lack of wine,
>
> your belly a heap of wheat
> surrounded with lilies.
>
> Your two breasts are two fawns,
> twins of a gazelle.
>
> Your neck is an ivory tower.
>
> Your eyes, the pools of Heshbon,
> by the gate of Bath-rabbim[10]

and the bride responds to the bridegroom in similar terms.

If there is no condemnation of sexual pleasure, it may be asked why extra-marital intercourse is condemned. The Decalogue and the various condemnations in Leviticus and Deuteronomy are concerned with the rights of the person. Sexual violation through adultery, fornication or even rape was an infringement of personal rights and according to one Scriptural scholar the fact that prohibition of adultery comes between murder and stealing points in this direction.[11] In a society where women were prize possessions, the violation of rights of father or husband was a serious matter. This is clearly demonstrated in this passage in Deuteronomy: 22:28

> If a man meets a virgin who is not betrothed and seizes and lies with her and is caught in the act, the man who has lain with her must give the girl's father fifty silver shekels: she shall be his wife since he has

violated her, and as long as he lives he may not repudiate her.

It is perfectly tenable to go beyond the Old Testament concepts of proprietary rights to interpret in our day and time fornication and adultery in terms of the potential damage to the integrity of human relationship. In either case the accent is not on the presence of illicit pleasure but on the well-being of the individual, the couple and society.

The New Testament

Despite everything that has been said about the New Testament, there is nothing in it which annuls this view of human sexuality.

Our Lord showed immense compassion to sexual frailty but never compromises on sexual integrity. He reminds his audience of the pristine ideal of life-long indissoluble marriage and proclaims the relatively new principle of the single state in the service of God. Those who wish to devalue the erotic and the sexual in general will quote Christ's saying that lustful, visual desire is as guilty as the adulterous action. But by no stretch of imagination can this be interpreted as an attack on the sexual. On the contrary, Our Lord is here going beyond the pragmatic exposition of the law to the depths of human reality in which integrity of relationship, the care and respect for another, belongs to one's inner world of motive and intention as much as the consequent action.

St Paul has also been portrayed as a detractor of sexuality. If all his writings are integrated and reviewed together, such a criticism is indefensible.

Christian Tradition

In the centuries that followed, the ideas of glorifying God in the body through sexual fulfilment faded into oblivion and a sexual pessimism overcame Christians which, despite several challenges, remained at the very heart of the Christian orientation. The reasons for this change from Jewish optimism are not easy to define. They certainly include Christianity's need to confirm the single state in the service of God, the influence of Greek thought, which saw the soul imprisoned in the body, and the impact of certain heresies like Gnosticism and Manichaeism which denied marriage as a child-related institution.

The following centuries are a happy hunting ground for those who wish to attack the Christian attitude to sexuality. The quotations from various Fathers are described in a scholarly way in *The Man-Woman Relationship in Christian Thought* by D. S. Bailey.[12] Christian thought finally crystallized with St Augustine, who settled for an approach highly inimical to sexual pleasure and a justification of sexual intercourse based on the *raison d'être* of procreation. This is not the place to describe in any detail how the views of St Augustine have been progressively modified over the centuries.[13]

Sufficient to say that although the general attitude to sexual pleasure has become increasingly less hostile Christianity has been left with an obsessional preoccupation with its dangers and has given very little attention to its positive characteristics.

Indeed, the alienation between sexuality and Christianity is best demonstrated by the fact that all the major advances in the last two centuries concerned with the subject have been basically initiated outside the Christian

Churches. Woman's emancipation, the drive to bring procreation under human control, sexual education with its emphasis on restoring attention to the beauty and goodness of sexuality, and the scientific study of sex in psychological terms have all emanated from outside the Christian tradition and encountered deep opposition from it. Compared to its initiative and work in education, its caring for the sick and the deprived, in the sphere of sexuality all that Christianity has managed to achieve until very recently is to condemn some of the inevitable short-comings of the innovations.

The time is long overdue for Christianity to take the initiative in this area. A faith committed to an understanding and realisation of love cannot leave sexuality out of its reckoning to the tender mercy of others. Christianity needs to affirm afresh the positive significance of sexuality and the erotic, and to indicate convincingly that the realisation of such a goal is perfectly consistent with the Good News. It needs to define afresh the meaning of human relationships in contemporary terms, using knowledge from the sciences of psychology, sociology, anthropology and biology, and to integrate the findings in the service of the Christian commandments which insist on loving God, our neighbour and ourselves.

II

The Nature of Sexuality

UNTIL THIS CENTURY, sexuality was described in adult terms of primarily heterosexual attraction, leading to intercourse and procreation. Thus the emphasis was on heterosexuality, coitus, erotic pleasure and fertility, all of which tended to emphasise the biologically active post-pubertal features of sexuality.

One genius changed all this. Sigmund Freud dropped his bombshell in 1905 with his *Three Essays on the Theory of Sexuality*.[1] It is worth recalling the opening remarks of this remarkable essay.

'Popular opinion has quite definite ideas about the nature and characteristics of this sexual instinct. It is generally understood to be absent in childhood, to set in at the time of puberty in connection with the process of coming to maturity and to be revealed in the manifestations of an irresistible attraction exercised by one sex upon the other; while its aim is presumed to be sexual union, or at all events action leading in that direction. We have every reason to believe, however, that these views give a very false picture of the true situation. If we look into them more closely we shall find that they contain a number of errors, inaccuracies and hasty conclusions.'[2]

At the very beginning of the serious study of the

psychology of sex, the abnormal provided the opportunity for the study of the normal. But the abnormal sexual perversions had first to be accepted and not summarily condemned. Freud did just this, and uncovered a wealth of information. The traditional view could not possibly explain why the sexual object, that which attracted a person sexually, could be for a man as varied as an adult woman, a little girl, a little boy, a young boy, another man, a female undergarment, rubber, leather, an animal, or a dead body.

Having been able to overcome the repulsion and disgust associated with such activities, Freud was able to reach and study these patients and through them formulate an extremely original, if complicated and, in the light of our knowledge today, biased and incomplete, theory of human sexuality. This is the libido theory.

Libido is the term used for the energy attached specifically to the sexual instincts, an energy with which each person is biologically endowed and which manifests itself in the body in different ways in the course of development. Libido is regarded as an energy or force, contained within a self-enclosed system, functioning within an economy of retention and discharge. Libido can be attached to an object which can be a person or thing, real or imagined.

The libido theory postulates that sexual energy is situated in certain parts of the body and speaks of oral, anal and phallic phases of development. The human personality is said to develop out of the successful resolution of each phase.

These phases commence in the first year of life at the mouth with the obvious concentration on sucking, swallowing, mastication and the associated sensations of being touched, held, nursed and watching mother. Thus the lips become the first erotogenic zone and the bodily encounter between child and mother is charged with gratifying sexual sensations.

The oral phase is followed by the anal. Just as the mouth is the chief centre of pleasurable experience in the first year, in the second and third the centre of elimination, the anus, becomes the centre of pleasure.

Finally, in the fourth and fifth year libidinal energy is concentrated on the genitalia. This is described as the phallic phase. In this context Freud formulated his famous Oedipus Complex, in which he described the sexual attraction the young boy feels for his mother and only resists through fear of his father. This fear is experienced in terms of possible castration as the punishment for the attempt to take mother away. This threat is enough to remove such libidinal wishes and the boy identifies with the father, thus establishing the basis of his masculinity; and by the same process, a young girl identifies with the mother.

This is the whole of Freud's sexual theory. By the age of five or six the essential sexual orientation is established and, after a latency period, puberty merely activates the endocrinological changes- which allow the secondary sexual characteristics to initiate adult genital activity.

Freud's theories need constant revaluation. He established the existence of an infantile sexuality in terms of touch, appearance, bodily contact and the various orifices of the body. Nobody seriously disputes these observations nowadays. They clearly exist and form part of adult sexuality.

For Freud, anatomy is destiny. Furthermore, it is the male anatomy that really matters. Both these concepts have been seriously challenged. The environment in the form of parents plays a crucial role. This has been demonstrated scientifically by using those extremely rare cases of infants in which the external genitalia do not clearly delineate at birth the sex of the child. It has been shown that the child will adopt the orientation towards masculinity or femininity, called the gender role, assigned by the parents even if it is shown later on that this runs contrary to its biological make-up.[3]

Beyond Freud

Apart from such biological mistakes, recent studies have shown that the gender of a person can be moulded independently of the anatomy or physiology, provided sufficient parental pressure is exerted.[4] Thus a mother who wants a girl desperately may dress and treat her boy in such a way as to achieve the desired result, producing a partial explanation of some of the 'cross-dressing' phenomena seen in adults.

Recently a leading psychoanalyst, John Bowlby, has formulated a further and distinctly different theory.[5] 'In traditional psychoanalytic theory the existence of such a linkage (between infantile and adult sexual behaviour) is accounted for on the grounds that the two forms of behaviour, infantile and adult, are simply the different expressions of a single libidinal form. In this view linkage and influence are taken for granted; what needs explanation is the difference between the two forms of behaviour. In the new theory, by contrast, it is the difference between the two forms of behaviour that is taken for granted and what needs explanation is the linkage between them.'[6]

Bowlby would accept some aspects of orthodox Freudian infantile sexuality but would repudiate that adult genital sexuality has its origins and precursors in childhood.

But of equal importance is Bowlby's original theory of human attachment. According to this theory, the infant forms a unique attachment to the mother from the earliest moments of life through an interconnective series of visual, auditory and touch stimuli. It learns to recognise mother through her appearance, voice and touch, and in this way forms strong one-to-one bonds, experiencing acute anxiety if it is separated from her too quickly. This attachment is a specific pattern of behaviour to which we return throughout our lives whenever we form intimate affectionate bonds. Bowlby is saying that the link between childhood and adult sexuality is the mediation of a common pattern of behaviour, namely attachment – we attach ourselves to one person exclusively. The accompanying genital behaviour is considered a distinctly post-pubertal expression of sexuality and in no way anticipated in childhood.

It should be further stressed that the childhood attachment-pattern between child and parents extends beyond the biological need for survival which Bowlby traces and relates to other subhuman species. It is in this unique learning situation that the child acquires psychologically the feelings of being recognised, wanted and appreciated – all the experiences, in short, designated by the term 'love'. These become fundamental needs in all human relationships and particularly in the permanent one of marriage.

All the studies referred to have one theme in common: that adult sexuality is somehow linked with events in childhood, events which belong to the first few years of life. All the evidence points to the truth of this.

The Ground of Love

Summing up the various views, the following picture emerges. There are two basic patterns of human attraction and attachment. The first is experienced in childhood between ourselves and our parents – first mother and then father. It is mediated through a whole series of bodily encounters which form the basis of attachment and are collectively described in lay language as affection. Human affection thus requires the basic ingredients of the child-parent encounter: acceptance, reliability, continuity, predictability, intimacy and trust, gentleness, gratification of physical needs without undue delay, encouragement and support, and the stimulation of physical, intellectual and emotional growth. The same characteristics are repeated in the second and only other intimate experience for the overwhelming majority of human beings – the permanent relationship of marriage (however defined). Sexual attraction now becomes a new powerful means of forming attachment-behaviour but it is insufficient to sustain it without the presence of affection. *A truly human bond is the appropriate combination of sexuality and affection.* This is in fact the situation in marriage, in which the partners act towards one another as a continuing source of sustaining, healing and growth-promoting activity: sustaining each other physically and psychologically; healing the wounds of the defects of the first intimate relationship of childhood and encouraging one another to further growth. This growth is now no longer physical or basically intellectual. Both these capacities reach their peak usually before marriage. It is growth in personal terms in which spouses help one another to deepen their awareness of themselves, making themselves available in an ever-deepening realisation of their potential.

In Christian terms this potential is complete only when it recognises and responds to Christ's invitation to form a relationship with him and through him with the Father and the Spirit. Needless to say, such a relationship demands the recognition of all the human characteristics, including the specific sexual dimension.

III

Growing Towards Marriage

IT IS IN the area of premarital sexuality that the clash between the past and the present is most evident. Traditional Christian thinking has offered certain precise rules for conduct. Sexual intercourse was only legitimate within marriage and always wrong before. Those who sought sexual pleasure before marriage were considered to be pursuing clearly immoral behaviour and a casuistry emerged preoccupied with what is or is not permissible in erotic play, always with the underlying implicit and explicit condemnation of premarital sexual intercourse.

When pressed to rationalise the grounds for such rules, the first fundamental answer has been the Scriptural prohibition against fornication and adultery. For many no other explanation is needed. But if pressed further a familiar answer has been that the pleasure accompanying sex is the Creator's reward for the present of procreation. Further still the danger of pregnancy and disease will be offered. Independent of these specific points, a powerful deterrent has been a general feeling in society that goodness, cleanliness, purity and uprightness are to be associated with premarital chastity.

Those opposing the Christian tradition began their counter-attack. Marriage, they insisted, does not guarantee the presence of love or sexual fulfilment.

Christian teaching has condemned thousands of couples to life-long unions of misery because of a single slip. Sex is for pleasure — one author calls it 'the healthiest and most important sport'[1] — as well as for procreation. Anyway, contraception has now made it possible to separate the procreative from the pleasurable aspect and it is up to a couple to use their sexuality freely as they think fit. They have now been liberated from the dual threats of pregnancy and venereal disease, both of which can be avoided and, if necessary, terminated by abortion or appropriate treatment. The ultimate sexual freedom implies the possibility of contraceptive intercourse, with abortion and antibiotic treatment if the intentions of the couple are frustrated by accident.

All this appears to the Christian nothing short of preposterous madness. It is attacked on the grounds of hedonism, irresponsibility and folly. Dire warnings of the appalling consequences are reiterated at regular intervals, backed by figures for venereal disease, abortion, illegitimacy and marital breakdown.

Those who are not locked in spontaneous and passionate acrimonious exchanges have to attempt to define the shortcomings of both attitudes. Christianity's deep-rooted fear of erotic pleasure and obsessional preoccupation with its dangers is matched by the opposite approach which isolates the instinctual from the rest of the person and ignores the severe cost in terms of human suffering and loss of integrity in the so-called solutions of abortion, venereal disease treatment and provisions for the single mother and the fatherless child.

When people of goodwill are examining the same situation and arriving at different conclusions, it is necessary to pause and find out whether agreement can be reached on essentials. Adolescence, the period under examination, is now known to be one of the most complex phases of human growth. Erikson, the well-known American psychoanalyst, calls it a psycho-social moratorium.[2] It extends between puberty and the early twenties and the implications of premarital sexuality can only be understood by the most careful attention to detail.

As already noted in the second chapter of this book, the child establishes its basic ability to form affectionate, loving, instinctual bonds of attachment from birth onwards in a series of relationships with mother, father and other surrogate figures. Thus it reaches puberty equipped with, and in many ways determined in, the ability to form intense and unique one-to-one relationships.

With the advent of puberty there are widespread neuro-endocrinological changes in the body which bring forth the development of the secondary sexual characteristics. The already-existing capacity to form personal bonds is now powerfully reinforced by sexual attraction and genital union, which become two principal means by which human beings can reach one another and bridge their separate existence. Thus adult sexuality exists to serve human relationships and as always it is the integrity of the individual and of the couple which is of paramount importance. Sex must be the servant of this integrity not its detractor.

But who is to judge the criteria of such integrity? No judgement is possible until the facts are known and in what follows, a scheme of the multiple processes of adolescence is outlined.

The growth of human personality can best be summarised as a process of gradual separation between child and its parents which reaches its acme in adolescence when the young person detaches himself or herself from the parents. This detachment has physical, psychological and social components.

Physically, the young person has to cope with 'aloneness'. Physical aloneness is not of course reached for the first time in adolescence; it is a process that has been proceeding since childhood. Human integrity now requires the capacity of the person to cope with this independence without excessive anxiety and tension. The overwhelming majority achieve this, a small number do not. Sexual intercourse is one way of bridging the gap. It guarantees a certain amount of closeness and if someone is desperate for companionship any price may be paid. Pleasure is incidental, it may be present or not.

Psychologically, the crucial experience is anxiety about the separation just described. When the person is overwhelmed by the fear of standing alone emotionally, they have a number of alternatives. They can stay at home, they can leave home and live with someone who acts as a parent substitute, or enter a community or job which has the appearance of parental security and conformity, such as religious life, the Forces, or a paternalistic apprenticeship. Most of these arrangements are pursued with little conscious awareness of the reasons that dictate them. Hence the boy or girl who marries at fifteen, sixteen, seventeen, forced by a pregnancy or not, or just lives with another, is not infrequently working out such a personal predicament.

Sociologically, the young person needs to establish a separate set of social values from the parents in order to clarify and accentuate the difference between themselves and him or her. This may and does take the form of clashes on politics, religion, social and personal issues such as dress, habits, work and so on. One frequently vital difference nowadays is sexual attitudes, and sexual intercourse may be experienced for a variety of subtle and latent reasons. Curiosity may be one of them. Another may be the rebellious assertion of freedom, whether as an act of hostile aggression towards the parents or simply as the only way of asserting the difference between the two generations.

Becoming a Person

Having established the process of detachment, or concurrently with it, the adolescent asks, 'Who am I?' This is hardly ever phrased in a single question like this, but the underlying meaning is present in these years when one is not a child nor yet grown up but living in a society which no longer prescribes categorically for this period of transition.

Identity is a word used by the psychological sciences to describe the essence of sameness and continuity in the presence of accumulated experiences, conscious and unconscious, in the individual. Identity has also physical, emotional and social components.

Physically, the most important change is to be found in the bodily changes associated with post-pubertal sexuality. Sexual identity has of course itself social, emotional and physical characteristics, but of these the last one is clearly prominent. Here there is a standing challenge to Christianity over the matter of masturbation. Moralists have tended to look increasingly less severely on masturbation recently but clearly, so long as sexual pleasure is considered as intrinsically wrong outside the sexual act in marriage, the mitigating factors have to be found in the degree of freedom and responsibility in the individual. This begs the fundamental question whether or not masturbation is not an intrinsic part of human growth at this stage of human development, giving the individual a precise knowledge of his or her sexual identity. I am inclined to the view that this is precisely the case at this stage of development. Masturbation gives the person an intense awareness of bodily sexual identity and as such belongs intrinsically to the phase of growth at this stage. This is not to say that masturbation is appropriate in other periods of life when the sexual identity now discovered has to be used at the service of the marital relationship or in loving others in the single state.

Emotionally, young men or women who have successfully detached themselves from the parents remain for a period unsure of themselves, isolated, lonely, lacking in self-esteem. They have left school where their status had been clear to join a society which demands they should start at the bottom of the ladder. Discovering womanhood and manhood is full of perplexing uncertainties. It is not surprising that all this pushes adolescents into intense groups and cliques desperately seeking security and acceptance from peers. At times they inhabit an alienated world cut off from the immediate past of childhood and as yet unable to penetrate the settled expectations of the adult. It is a world in which emotional, physical and social deprivation is acutely experienced and it is through the ranks of the young that society receives powerful reminders of the needs of the deprived and rejected, the dual experiences felt so strongly in this period.

It is not surprising that those who feel the isolation and deprivation intensely will seek comfort from temporary sexual liaisons. Cut off from the love of parents, not ready to pursue the love of permanent relationship, they have only the temporary and transient from which to squeeze the last ounce of comfort, encouragement and support.

Socially, of course, the most precise form of identification is to be found in the work or profession to be pursued. These are the years of change and uncertainty in work and many a young person is presented with the uncertainty and discouragement of not knowing what to do. Once again the frustrations of such a situation can be temporarily mitigated by the reassurance of mattering to someone, even if it is for only one night and the other is a stranger.

Having made the separation, found a separate identity, the vast majority of people are now ready to form a new attachment within which intimacy will be expressed afresh. This is the stage of courtship and marriage. Sexual intercourse in this third and final phase takes on a very different meaning from the previous stages. Sexual intercourse now clearly belongs to a relationship in which re-attachment and commitment are the goals. And indeed, within the Christian tradition, we had a period when the Church accepted the validity of a marriage when a couple freely chose to commit and consummate their love in their first act of sexual intercourse. The evil of clandestine marriages, however – the mushrooming of situations in which a man promised to marry and consummated several 'marriages' in different places with several women – forced the Church to insist on a public ceremony with witnesses.

The need to safeguard individuals and to protect couples from the ensuing chaos is required as much today as it was in the late Middle Ages. The point, however, that is being emphasised is the increased appropriateness of sexual intercourse in these circumstances and the need to pursue a sympathetic and understanding approach when sex is anticipated in these circumstances.

The Moral Issues

In his excellent study, *The Sexual Behaviour of Young People*,[3] Michael Schofield indicated a round figure of some 350,000 boys and girls under the age of twenty in England and Wales as having experienced premarital intercourse. Instead of adopting a critical, judgemental and despairing approach, Christianity has to define afresh the relevant issues and offer possible constructive help to this sizeable minority.

Christians must ask whether it is permissible to lump all premarital sexual intercourse together and condemn it on a single principle of lowered moral standards reflecting a hedonism of the age. Any close examination of the subject makes such an approach naïve and irrelevant. The young close their ears to the drone of mournful incantations because they feel in their heart of hearts that Christianity does not understand their needs or, if it does, has not developed either a language of adequate communication or constructive assistance.

It is imperative to help young people to distinguish between integrity and exploitation. There are those who justify premarital sexual intercourse as the appropriate means of growth. Here Christianity must take a stand, not on the negative issue of eroticism, but on the positive one of human integrity. Does premarital sexual intercourse really serve the various phases of adolescent growth? Or is sexual intercourse used as a substitute solution for the inevitable difficulties that have to be faced in this period of formation? Is human integrity served when the body is used as an alternative for the capacity to grow up and to discover one's separate existence? How does one draw the distinction between love and mutual exploitation, when two people, frequently in ignorance, are using one another to negotiate a stage in their development – an experiment to be repeated again and again until they reach a point when they are capable of committing themselves permanently to somebody?

Human relationships are built on the principles of availability, continuity, reliability and predictability and these are conditions found in the parent-child relationship and in marriage. They guarantee the conditions for sustenance, growth and healing. Transient and casual affairs are saturated with characteristics of uncertainty, anxiety, living constantly with fear of loss and absence of the stability which is the necessary foundation for the development of human relationships. Christianity has to show again that sexual intercourse is the personal gift through which two people seal privately and publicly the commitment of their whole self to each other. Until they are ready to do this, sexual intercourse cannot be anything else than a partial expression of themselves and is much more often a means of negotiating some other aspect of their life. It is this devaluation of sexuality's unique significance that must be attacked – but in constructive and helpful terms. This means that people of all ages, facing these difficulties in their single state, need to receive from the Christian community the help that can recognise and identify their problem, and be given the individual attention which can encourage them to grow without needing to compromise the integrity of their own sexuality or that of others.

IV

Sexuality in Marriage

'FOR THIS REASON, a man must leave his father and mother and be joined to his wife and the two will become one body. This mystery has many implications; but I am saying it applies to Christ and the Church.'[1]

This is a passage which gives two monumental theological insights. First, the theology of adolescence – the detachment-separation, identity formation and re-attachment referred to in the previous chapter – is clearly hinted at by St Paul, who himself is referring to the text in Genesis specifying the separation of the man from the parents. That this applied equally to the woman is implicit in the passage, but it needed the feminine emancipation of our age to clarify the point. Secondly, the physical union of the spouses now symbolises and reflects the total commitment of Christ to his Body, the Church. This commitment is saturated totally with availability, continuity, reliability and predictability, the same characteristics that define the essential ingredients for integrity and love in human relationships.

Thus the monogamous fidelity of marriage which the Judaeo-Christian tradition has expressed as the ideal goal for human beings can now be seen in terms of what within which human beings may best find the means for human integrity requires. It specifies the conditions survival, healing and growth. Fidelity has to be examined in these terms rather than those of sexual indiscretion and erotic pleasure.

At the beginning of an article like this on sexuality in marriage, for example, the question that has to be faced is the morality of trial marriages. Here apparently is the ideal answer of contemporary wisdom. Two people, we are told, need to get to know each other before they undertake marriage. They have to discover whether they are suited to one another physically and psychologically. Contraception (in theory) takes care of the unwanted child. The situation is now ready for experiment. This is so eminently sensible. What is wrong with it?

Only this. Two people are telling each other: 'I am not sure of myself or of you. I am neither ready nor do I know how to give you the whole of myself. I need to have permanently an escape door. You have to live with the possibility that you will attach yourself to me but I am free to abandon you without having to justify myself. You have no right to build any expectations on me, nor have I on you. We can unilaterally abandon one another as and when it becomes necessary.'

The reason why the idea of trial marriage fails is clear from the consequences of such a situation. Human integrity in relationships requires continuity, reliability, predictability. All relationships have to face the problems of conflict, aggression and alienation which are the other side of the coin of harmony, unity and love. Continuity is needed to resolve conflict through forgiveness and reparation, and through the growth of mutual understanding to avoid further conflict.

To continuity must be added reliability against the anxiety of loss, the fear of being abandoned. It is not possible really to be human and thrive under the continued threat of losing and restarting intimate relationships.

Finally, to continuity and reliability we need some measure of predictability. We function largely on the familiar, the known and the predictable; otherwise life would come to a standstill. The mutual sharing of the spouses is the fount of further development on a basis of experiences shared and realised together.

The Context of Love

This is of the greatest importance in marriage, with so many vital and unrepeatable 'first' events such as the pregnancy and birth of each child, individual milestones, the crucial experiences of personal loss and triumph, as well as the biological and psychological phenomena of illness and changes such as the menopause. These are experiences which provide the accumulated store of predictable knowledge about oneself and another person that is one of the foundations for safe-guarding human beings from much anxiety of the unknown. They cannot be relived with any other human being. Every time a new relationship of intimacy has to be established, the past, with all its accumulated richness and suffering, has to be conveyed afresh to a recipient who can only receive it with all the handicaps of being absent from the actual events. In some instances this is an advantage, but very often it means that little can be taken for granted and much energy has to be expended explaining afresh. That, in a life of a limited span and opportunity, is surely a handicap.

Christianity can in fact turn the tables on those who seek trial marriages. It can ask them why, considering the obvious advantages of permanency and stability, they should reject these. If the dialogue is free from acrimonious charges and countercharges which confine everybody to rigid defensive positions, it can be shown that those who see trial marriages in the name of sexual freedom have not reached the stage in their own development when they can relate to each other without requiring an escape door. Only with an escape route freely available can they relate at all and not become overwhelmed with anxiety. Similarly, it can be agreed that if Christian marriage is simply a means of chaining together two people who cannot use the conditions of monogamy to form a minimum relation in which their human needs for sustenance, healing and growth are met, then no marriage exists.[2][3]

Given that a life-long commitment is the most apt expression within which the spouses and the children can do justice to their whole personality, what is the specific role of sexuality itself? This is another critical issue for Christianity, which has hitherto focused its attention, on the procreational potential of sexuality. The limitations of such an approach do not imply any criticism of the attitude itself, which has expressed adequately a part of the truth; but there can be no doubt that it is only a part of the truth.

So far, in these chapters, it has been shown that both erotic and sexual pleasure are intrinsically valuable and good human experiences, provided they serve the integrity of the individual and the appropriate human relationship. It has also been shown that sexual attraction and genital consummation are two of the most powerful means of reinforcing the attachment of two people to one another.

This is what has come to be described as the 'enosis-potential' of sexuality, its power to unify the two

SEXUALITY IN MARRIAGE

partners. Traditionally, Christianity has chosen to emphasise marriage's procreative potential.

These two approaches can now be compared. As far as the procreation potential is concerned, the physiology of the body sets its own limits to what is possible. Fertilisation is possible only once a month in a short period of five to six days which for most people is a predictable event.[4] Thus the overwhelming majority of sexual acts have no procreative potential: such is the specific design of the Creator. Furthermore, procreation ends at the menopause and, given the modern advances in medicine, couples can expect on average at least another twenty years of married life in which sexual relations continue, albeit with diminished frequency.[5] Thus it is abundantly clear that procreation is not the characteristic which is intrinsically present in each act of sexual intercourse. Are there any features which are potentially present in each act of sexual intercourse?

In order to answer this question, it is important to recall that there are essentially only two intimate relationships in life, that between the child and its parent, particularly the mother, and that between husband and wife, both of which relations are in turn symbols of that between man and God.

Now in the first year of life most babies have, in the arms of the mother, the bodily experience of closeness, warmth, safety and instinctual satisfaction. It is through the body that we acquire the first experiences of trust, without which there can be no survival. In the next few years the child progresses beyond this bodily closeness and trust, and experiences at a distance the feelings of being recognised, wanted, appreciated, the sum total of what we call affection and love. But it is bodily closeness that provides the means by which the child is relieved of discomfort and pain and receives reassurance. This rescue from hunger and discomfort has been described by Melanie Klein, a famous British psychoanalyst, as the first 'repeated consolatory experience of life'[6].

It is my contention that sexual intercourse in marriage is the continuation of these repeated consolatory experiences. Freud and some traditional elements in Christianity are both wrong in seeing the instinctual as having the primacy of significance, positively or negatively, in sexual intercourse. On the contrary, the instinctual now becomes the single most powerful means of serving and verifying the attachment of the couple. Through it, mutual trust, recognition, acceptance, appreciation and reconciliation – in short, love – are communicated. This loving, uniting potential is indubitably the only characteristic that is present in every act of sexual intercourse in marriage and the quality that needs fostering all the time since it lies at the very heart of the relationship. Only in the presence of such embryonic and growing love can the sexual act be used in its other biological potentiality. We have now reached the stage when the couple can decide the most suitable timing for their love to become specifically fertile, having given consideration to all their circumstances. Certainly every new life has the right to be conceived in conditions in which it can receive the unconditional love of its parents.

Christ's Response to Adultery

Having outlined the positive aspects of marital sexuality, what can be said of adultery? One thing is clear: it receives unequivocal condemnation in the Scriptures, both in the Old[7] and the New Testaments.[8] It is

SEXUALITY IN MARRIAGE

also the occasion of one of the most moving and compassionate moments in the gospel of St John, when Christ is confronted with the scribes and Pharisees over the woman caught committing adultery.[9] How can we reconcile these two pronouncements? Even more important, what can Christianity's attitude be to a contemporary world which, if not actually encouraging adultery, does not actively condemn it?

It was noted in the first chapter that one aspect of the condemnation of adultery in the Old Testament was the violation of personal and proprietary rights of the spouse. In some ways this concept has remained and forms one of the basic grievances of the spouse whose partner has committed adultery, the feeling of violation of their rights. Something which they consider belongs to them has been lost temporarily or permanently to someone else. There is a sense of having had something stolen.

When marriage was conceived merely in contractual terms, these feelings reflected accurately the sense of personal loss. As marriage moves away from being considered a contract and is now experienced increasingly as a relationship, adultery calls for a different evaluation. There is a need to go beyond the violation of a contract to a deeper understanding of why such a violation has taken place.

Adultery can now be seen as a symptom in a marriage when the minimum needs of one or two people are not being met. This concept of the minimum need evokes deep opposition from those who think only in terms of an abstract concept of the common good and ignore the reality of individual needs. In fact, the common good is based on the progressive and growing realisation of the human potential of individual couples. Few are likely to risk lightly the considerable anxieties, dangers and conflicts entailed in an affair with another person. If couples are experiencing a minimum contentment of their needs, they are likely to remain faithful to one another, they need no one else to complete their lives and if good communication exists they can work out problems as they emerge. Where their minimum needs are not being met and no channels of communication exist to reach one another, then adultery is a cry for help arising from the depths of a tottering relationship.

Adultery is thus either a cry for help or the sign of the death or non-existence of a relationship. Its significance has little to do with the enjoyment of illicit pleasure outside the matrimonial bond, and millions of individual acts of adultery have given testimony to the fact that the shock can arrest the downward path of the disintegration of a marriage if reconciliation is still possible. This is of course in no way a recommendation of adultery as a short-cut to marital counselling. A couple should seek help long before they have reached this situation.

> He looked up and said: 'Woman, where are they? Has no one condemned you?' 'No-one, Sir,' she replied.
>
> 'Neither do I condemn,' said Jesus, 'go away and don't sin any more.'

Our Lord himself gives us the answer as to how to respond to adultery. With his Divine wisdom he could look into the hearts of men and women with all the skill of modern psychiatry and much more. He thus avoided the tempting superficial conclusions and judgements. He did not condemn the adulteress; that is to say, he did not reject her in a torrent of legislative condemnation. But he also made it quite clear that she had to go away and sin no more; that is to say, become more fully human, live more fully the image of God in herself.

That is precisely what the Christian response to adultery must be. It should be the signal to examine the quality of a marriage: to find out whether a marriage really exists or not and if it does, however minimally, to help the couple in every possible way to restore their marital relationship. As far as Christians are concerned this need for reconciliation and further mutual growth is an obligation, not a choice, but here Christianity is expressing the necessity to keep a marriage and family intact if at all possible, a goal which ultimately expresses human integrity.

V

Children

'BY THEIR VERY nature, the institution of matrimony itself and conjugal love are ordained for the procreation and education of children and find in them their ultimate crown.'[1]

Countless generations of Catholics, as indeed of all Christians, have grown up with this sentence and its analogies reverberating in the fabric of their personality. Marriage was for children and in a language that lasted hundreds of years and is now buried overnight in the Vatican II declaration, children and their education was the primary end of marriage. Any hint to the contrary, any modification was construed as a fundamental attack on the nature of marriage, hence the massive hostility shown to birth control which was initially interpreted as an 'anti-baby' campaign. So long as the understanding and theology of marriage concentrated entirely on children to the exclusion of its other facets, it is perfectly understandable that any threat to this understanding evoked marked anxiety. And yet within a few decades the situation has altered radically through a variety of social and psychological factors.

First of all the impact of medicine in terms of modern obstetrics has revolutionised child-bearing. The total infant mortality (death of a child under one year) in 1911 was calculated to be 129.4 per 1000 live births.[2] The corresponding figure in 1968 was 18.7: a sevenfold decrease.[3] Similarly the number of children born dead (stillbirths) was nearly halved between 1930 and 1960 to just under 20 per 1000 live births. Finally, the majority of women (eighty-five per cent) can expect to complete the pregnancy they have commenced successfully.[4] Thus the desired size of family can now be produced with little risk to the life or health of either mother or child, and the control achieved over the process of procreation is a truly monumental advance. Wives have been relieved of a great deal of hardship and misery from repeated pregnancies and the massive waste of infant life which was the natural expectation until very recently. This has meant the freeing of the overwhelming majority of sexual activities in marriage from procreative purposes. The beginning of the fertile phase at a much earlier age in a woman's life has almost meant one or more decades of married life without necessarily the single most familiar activity of the past, i.e. 'bearing and rearing'. A view of marriage so heavily devoted to procreation and, in particular to the number of children, finds itself at a loss as to how to respond to a totally changed situation. The answer, however, is very clear. The emphasis has to shift, as far as children are concerned, from quantity, from sheer *number*, to quality, and this implies a thorough understanding of the parental role in the education of children. But before turning to this, mention should be made of the childless couple.

Childless Couples

The infertile couple used to hold a peculiar position in Christianity. Infertility was no barrier to marriage but clearly such was the significance of children that childless couples must often have wondered what their status was in the Christian community unless they could rectify their barrenness or adopt. Today, of course, infertility is being tackled with increasing success but there still remains the couple who cannot have children. Modern research is showing, incidentally, that this is a problem to which either husband or wife may contribute. Male sterility, complete or partial, is just as important as a wife's infertility. There is, of course, the possibility of adoption, and this can be a perfect solution.

But there still remains yet another group of marriages in which the partners are fertile but do not wish to have children. Apart from rare genetic conditions which are dangerous or unwise for procreation, a couple may decide for valid reasons not to have children. Such a decision was and is still likely to be interpreted as selfish and irresponsible. The inevitable conclusion is that being so self-centred they are not prepared to open themselves to a new life. This can certainly happen but as with all these apparently self-evident moral conclusions a little further consideration will disclose other aspects. Childbearing, procreation and children have certainly their bleak, painful moments but for the parents, and particularly the mother, they express the realisation of a potential that is basic to human nature biologically, psychologically and sociologically. It is an achievement that has immediate status and recognition. Its absence is a loss and people do not seek lightly their own belittlement. Whenever human nature is stamped with the quality of selfishness it is always worth looking a little further.

What will be found is common knowledge to those working intimately in this area. There are women, many women, who are petrified by the whole process of childbearing. Their refusal to contemplate it is no stubborn withdrawal from responsibility but the expression of their inner desperate panic. Fear, panic, immaturity: these are the characteristics which contribute to the refusal. Frequently such women themselves do not comprehend the reasons for their behaviour and live with an unwarranted sense of guilt. This may well be one reason, then, for an apparent selfishness in this respect, but what happens when whole countries adopt such an attitude, however legitimate the causes? Is it not possible that the human population may in the end be decimated for psychological reasons? Such fears do exist and they cannot be ignored.

At the present moment, however, overpopulation is a much more urgent peril than the disappearance of the human race through selfish withdrawal from procreation. Every country, every nation, has to decide on the balance between reproducing itself and concentrating on the quality of the life of its members. If there are not enough members born in replacement then the nation will disappear, though it is likely that long before this happens a reversing action will occur. There is also an inbuilt tension between the gratification of childbearing and raising a family, and the alternative of non-childbearing, social and intellectual goals. It is by no means self-evident that the latter are that much stronger than the former.

Behind all these nihilistic contemplations lies the fear that sexual pleasure which is not channelled to procreation is bound to run amok and create chaos in human society. Such a fear neither understands the rich potential of human sexuality nor recognises the innate responsibility of human nature which while it has unlimited capacity for destruction and disintegration has also an equal capacity for creative and imaginative development of its potential. It seems to me incompatible with the Christian faith not to side with the forces of hope and confidence in man's capacity to respond to the image of God whose perfection he is trying to realise.

If a couple, knowing their sensitivities and limitations decide against having children, then in all probability they are making the right decision in their own special circumstances provided they seek the appropriate advice and help. It is infinitely better that their relationship should survive intact and become stable than that everybody should suffer, including the child, whose presence will become a continuous threat to the survival of the marriage.

The relationship of the parents

The decision against procreation cannot be taken lightly and needs constant reviewing with one crucial factor in mind, namely the stability of the parental relationship. Christian teaching has always coupled procreation with education of the child. Unfortunately the stress was laid far too strongly on the former than on the latter of which the meaning has deepened and extended in the last few decades. 'Education' is much more than simply meeting the physical and educational needs of the child. It is a great deal more than providing adequate food, shelter, clothing and the Catholic school. These are necessary background requirements but the atmosphere and the quality of the relationship between the child and its parents is infinitely more important. Perhaps the single greatest advance in our understanding of education in this century concerns the vital importance of the early years for the emotional maturity of the developing personality. Men and women can grow up with the finest intellectual education and be materially unaware of what deprivation is, but they can still be vulnerable, handicapped human beings unable to initiate or sustain a relationship of love with others. Hence the emphasis is shifting from quantity, from sheer numbers to quality and the ultimate test of this as far as Christianity is concerned is the individual's capacity to love his neighbour and himself, a reality which is first learned at home.

We love others because we were first loved ourselves by our parents, hence the indisputable necessity for the presence of stable parents capable of communicating to their children this precious quality.

The nature of love

No parent is perfect and no child is capable of learning all that it receives from its parents. What is desirable is a mutual matching of giving and receiving, but in these early years, the timing is critical. The early years of life are the ones which find the child most helpless, dependent and in need of loving care. Physical caring is essential and the battered baby syndrome has revealed a widespread problem in which the mother unleashes on her child violence instead of love. From this extreme there is to be found all gradations of rejection and neglect which are not always the mother's fault. Not infrequently she finds herself in a predicament which is beyond her capacity to bear.

The deprivation can be relative in which the parents are willing but incapable of understanding their child's special needs, thus remaining aloof, or mistakenly they overprotect it and smother its road of independence.

These psychological needs of trust, security, autonomy,

initiative, the fostering of competence and independence, frighten and intrigue a new generation of parents. The cynics comment that people got along well enough before. The real answer is that this is a half-truth. Where these characteristics were fostered the results were, as might be expected, satisfactory. The casualties, and there were many, were labelled in some terms of moral disapproval; everyone had a convenient scapegoat solution. Today such answers are no longer acceptable. With care and foresight the potential damage inflicted on children can be reduced; our growing understanding of the processes involved permit both anticipation and effective intervention. Everyone can gain and no one need suffer from the ever deepening understanding of man's nature. We are still at the very beginning of this process and no doubt mistakes of emphasis and evaluation will be made. But these should not mean a return to the habits of the past where intellect, body and emotions were isolated from one another with the latter virtually ignored.

The parent-child relationship is a process of gradual evolution culminating in adolescence where the young man or woman emerges as a separate person. During these vital first two decades we acquire the most significant experiences of our lives through which we learn to feel recognised, wanted, appreciated, in short the essentials of love. In turn we acquire a capacity to trust ourselves, experience our worthiness, feel our goodness, and can offer it to others. The acquisition of these qualities gives us the discerning capacity to relate to ourselves and to others and it is not exaggeration to state that herein lies the single most important event of our lives.

Hence the increasing importance attached to these years. The task of the parents is long, arduous and vital.[5] They need encouragement and help, and here the community and parish as a whole, the school, relatives and friends, all play important supporting roles. But it is the parents who will lay the foundations of the meaning of love, the principal significance of which will be trust and faith, faith in them and through them to God, the source of all faith.

VI

Sexual Deviations

PERHAPS NOWHERE MORE than in the area of sexual deviation has the Christian attitude shown such alienation from its roots of compassion and love without which the Good News becomes a fossilised, legalistic statement of prohibitions.

Sexual deviation is a difficult concept to define, because the criteria of sexual normality vary from age to age and amongst different societies. Nevertheless, it is safe to assume that within this category would be included all the practices which evoke sexual arousal and gratification other than heterosexually and in the normal apposition of the genitalia.

In order to classify sexual deviation a little more clearly, we have to use certain psychological terms. The word 'object' stands for the person or thing which excites sexually. This is normally a woman for a man and vice versa. Taking the case of the man, he can in fact be excited sexually by another man, young boy or child of either sex, and by a whole series of inanimate objects such as female undergarments, rubber, leather or any other smooth object. In the more extreme condition animals can become substitute objects. These conditions are called homosexuality, fetishism and bestiality respectively. Of these homosexuality is undoubtedly the commonest condition and will be considered further below.

In another set of abnormalities the man may wish to dress in feminine clothes or wear feminine undergarments, a condition called transvestism, or in rare occasions desire to change sex completely and become a woman, which has been called transexualism.

Within the range of heterosexuality, deviation may be present in those who find it impossible to come close to a real woman and can only experience gratification at a distance by watching. This is voyeurism, the cause of the not uncommon problem of Peeping Toms. It is also at the root of pornography, which stimulates visually without requiring the presence of a real person.

Much more commonly in either homosexual or heterosexual relationships the participants desire either to inflict pain, suffering or humiliation on their partner, which is called sadism, or to experience it, which is called masochism. Variants of sado-masochism are perhaps some of the more frequent aspects of sexual deviation.

These are some of the commoner manifestations of sexual deviation as far as the sexual object is concerned. The sexual aim may also be widely divergent.

The sexual aim may be simply sexual arousal with or without gratification. It may proceed to orgasm with or without masturbation or coitus. Sexual pleasure may be experienced in isolation or in the presence of others, in fantasy or reality.

Apart from sexual deviations themselves, all societies have recognised the presence in their midst of the oldest profession, that of the prostitute, and her clients.

Until recently all this was hardly mentionable publicly in respectable circles and certainly found little official recognition and sympathy in Christianity apart from the isolated pockets of care given by religious communities to those who sought help. Those who experienced these difficulties very often felt the full opprobrium of condemnation, shame and disgust which their conditions evoked. Not infrequently they considered themselves as a peripheral fringe-group which belonged to the collective garbage of unmentionables. It was Havelock Ellis, Sigmund Freud and others, repudiating God and the Church, who did not repudiate the suffering, misery and isolation of these human beings. They were prepared to examine closely and describe in detail these problems, thus laying the foundations for the modest beginnings of present-day treatment based on psycho-analytical and learning theory.

How did Christianity manage to steer itself away so far from the roots of Him who was the friend of tax collectors and sinners?

Certainly the deep-seated fear of sexuality meant that everything which smacked of the subject had to be approached with caution and at a distance. Secondly, the fear of contamination meant that the common-good morality was pursued with sincerity. The deep conviction that hard cases made bad law was maintained even if it flew in the face of one of the basic principles of Christianity – Our Lord's concern for the one sheep which went astray.

But one wonders if those who were prepared to treat the problems of the few harshly for the sake of the good of the majority had any idea of how many the few were. Modern epidemiological studies have examined several of these problems in detail. Making allowances for the difficulty in obtaining accurate figures it is possible that in Great Britain there may be as many as a million homosexual men[1] and half a million women[2]. Furthermore, modern psychological knowledge suggests that it is inappropriate to divide normality abruptly from abnormality.

In other words, there is in all of us the potential, embryonically at least, to behave in abnormal ways. These traits are quantitatively distributed in the population. The traits exist consciously and/or unconsciously to a variable degree. There can be no separation of 'we' and 'they'. The only thing to do is to recognise this and deal with our own individual tendencies in a way that will best respect the whole integrity of our personality and that of others.

If we refuse to do so, if we reject that bit of ourselves as unacceptable, if we split it off from the centre of our being, then we shall similarly reject the tendency in others with double disapproval because its presence in them threatens to awaken what is dangerous and threatening within ourselves. One consequence of this is the ferocity with which such sufferers are attacked and condemned. Rationalised on different grounds, the condemnation, then, is in fact frequently based on the individual and collective fear that this problem will touch and awaken the enemy within ourselves or the community.

Our Lord had no part of himself which needed rejection and thus there was no part of others which demanded his rejection of them as people. No one was a threat, which made it possible for him to come close to everyone, to reach them and to help them restore integrity to their whole self. The Church, which is his Body, has to seek in the fullness of time the same goal and, as far as sexual deviation is concerned, the time is now appropriate to take a fresh look at this topic.

The Roots of Promiscuity

Even if the sexual deviations are foreign to some people, no one is unaware that promiscuous behaviour exists and that it has received the unequivocal condemnation of Christianity. Indeed, the most widespread fear held about our age is its tendency to sanctify promiscuity and sexual permissiveness.

As things stand, the man or woman who persistently acts in a promiscuous manner has been the target of the most clear condemnation for his or her lascivious behaviour. On the surface the situation is clear-cut. These people pursue pleasure for its own sake, admit it and in our permissive society boast about it and encourage others to experience it. Indeed a few do all this, but let us pause for a moment.

Why does a man or woman behave like this? 'For pleasure,' is the answer: what more is needed to answer the question? In fact much more. We have noted the human advantages of stable, continuous relationships which allow secure bonds of affection, security and personal love to be developed. Now these men and women are deliberately depriving themselves of all this. They and everyone else will rationalise it on the basis of excitement, the need for change and the freedom to enjoy uninhibited pleasure.

On closer examination the personality of such men and women shows a whole set of different characteristics. They are frequently timid, extremely anxious people, unable to form any close and stable relationships. Deep within themselves they carry the trait of mistrust and fear which makes it impossible for them to trust or feel safe with anyone beyond the merest casual contact. They have no self-esteem and are concerned that no one wants them. They are convinced that they possess little that is lovable within themselves which others could want to share with them.

Normally every sexual act in a happy marital relationship is preceded and followed by an ongoing human relationship. The prostitute and her client come together precisely because neither of them can establish such continuous human relationship. The comfort which one or the other receives from the temporary union of their bodies is an accurate reflection of the poverty of their personality, only a fragment of which can be shared fractionally with another human being. Far from deserving our condemnation, these are some of the more vulnerable, deprived and rejected of human beings, subject to the tyrannies of their own acute limitations and the exploitation of others. In the heart of promiscuity, just as with drug addiction and alcoholism, lies utter and complete human loneliness and isolation, crying out to be reached as the victims themselves are often past the point of being able to save themselves.

The Positive Approach

Some of the deviations, such as looking, touching, fetishism and sadomasochism, can be easily understood as continuations in adulthood of the remnants of infantile sexuality as described by Freud. The eye and physical contact are the first means of experiencing pleasure in the body. If a person is unable for one reason or another to progress beyond this, they remain fixed at this libidinal stage of development.

Fetishism, the term used to describe the substitution of some inanimate object for a human being, also indicates the inability of the person to reach and feel safe in close proximity to a real person. In these circumstances fantasy, the substitute use of these objects, and pornography are the only possibilities open to such people.

Another explanation to account for such behaviour is based on the Pavlovian learning theory which eschews psychoanalytical theory. According to this view, the person acquires these tendencies simply because at some critical moment some particular object or situation evoked a strong enough pleasurable sensation, the way to obtain which was learned, acquired and repeated thereafter.

The single largest sexual deviation encountered in our society is, by far, homosexuality, and more needs to be said about it. Extensive research has so far yielded little unequivocal explanation for its cause. Studies have suggested that genetic factors[3] and the family milieu[4] both contribute towards it.

Studies of male homosexuals have statistically shown the presence of a parental configuration with the presence of a prominent, dominating, assertive mother and an inconspicuous, shadowy, passive, non-prominent or absent father. A recent British study of lesbians[5,6] also suggests a markedly disturbed family background with a greater incidence of marital disruption through separation and divorce.

The family constellation provides the most clear basis on which sexual identity is developed. The boy needs a father-figure to learn to be a man and similarly a girl needs a mother-figure. Furthermore, the boy needs to be able safely to approach and form bonds of affection with the mother as the basis of heterosexual relationships later on, and similarly the girl needs to be able safely to approach and form bonds of affection with the father.

SEXUAL DEVIATIONS

The absence of these ingredients, in their extreme form, undoubtedly influences the sexual orientation of the children.

Here Christianity is faced with a straightforward choice. So far it has attempted to influence sexual integrity by associating condemnation, shame, disapproval and taboo with sexual deviations. In doing so it has inevitably at times tended to forget that the goal is human integrity, not an obsessional preoccupation with the dangers of sexual pleasure itself.

So far it has used the instruments of shame, fear and punishment as its main weapons to fight deviation. These are indiscriminate and decreasingly efficient means, and they certainly do not do justice to the Christian commandment of loving our neighbour, for in rejecting the part, there is a real danger of rejecting the whole person.

There is a need to examine each of these problems individually and to try to understand the biological, psychological and social determinants of each and offer appropriate help to restore human integrity. In doing so Christianity must be much more concerned to promote growth of the whole person than to suppress the surface phenomena of individual acts.

It is human growth towards wholeness that must be the ultimate aim. Personal growth, leading the person to move on from transient, casual, ineffectual relationships to the formation of more stable and permanent friendships, is clearly one aim of wholeness.

Christianity must indeed proclaim unequivocally the norm of heterosexuality but will have to accept that for a few homosexuality is a fixed and unalterable state. For such individuals the negative advice hitherto given which merely prohibits physical sexual contact can in no way be considered a sufficient approach to the development of personal growth and stable relationships.

Each problem will have to be examined individually, and help on a much vaster and expert level be available, if the appropriate progress, which is infinitely more than the mere avoidance of sexual contact, is to be made. Here as elsewhere, Christianity needs to lose its fear of the sexual and face the whole person with his or her multiple needs, encouraging the slow progress towards human integrity. In this the advances of modern psychological treatment are indispensable but so is the will of the individual to reach personal integrity.

Christianity has been afraid that if it drops prohibitions, human beings will go to pieces, and be left to the mercy of hedonism. While the dangers exist, this attitude seriously ignores the innate tendency towards wholeness which human beings have. It is this basic human aspiration which Christianity must make its principal goal. It has to identify it, however minimal, in the individual, and reinforce it with encouragement and positive therapy rather than resorting to threats and fear.

VII

The Single State

IN A CENTURY increasingly conscious of the significance of sexuality and marriage, the place of the single person has become less defined and uncertain. A brief look at the Registrar General's statistics shows the increasing popularity of marriage, especially amongst young people. For example, at the turn of the century 18 men in every 1,000 under twenty were married. In 1968 the same figure had grown to 90; for women the same figures are respectively 92 and 288.[1] The popularity of marriage and remarriage remains undiminished.

Christianity is faced with two challenges. The first is to deepen its understanding of the single person who for one reason or another remains unmarried and the second is to examine afresh the significance of the single state dedicated to God. As far as the latter is concerned, it is imperative to go beyond the emotional outbursts between those who defend the state and insist on its continuation and those who seek freedom to discharge their religious duties in whatever state they think fit. One of the most distressing aspects of the contemporary scene in the Church is to watch the charges and countercharges on various issues which involve the Pope and the bishops personally in attacking or defending a particular position. Perhaps few popes and bishops have had a more challenging task than Paul VI and the various hierarchies, and what they need from all of us is constructive help to clarify the issues. No justice is done to them or the

Church in making personal statements the target for blasts and counter-blasts which by-pass serious discussion, free from personal animosity.

The worst fears of Christianity seem to be confirmed in the ever-growing literature dedicated to the sex life of the single person. Presumably in order to redress the injustice of the double standards of the past, advice is offered particularly to the single woman. The sex life of the college, university, office or factory girl is at the receiving end of millions of words of advice, most of which are not worth the paper on which they are written. In spite of all this, the woman who, through no fault of her own, finds herself single and is surrounded by the fulfilment, apparent or real, of her married sister, can very understandably respond with the twin feelings of envy and jealousy.

For those taken up with the idea of sexual gratification isolated from an authentic human relationship, the problem is relatively easy: namely, how to pursue sexual fulfilment without being involved in the risks of pregnancy and disease. These people rely on the added protection of abortion and specific treatment if needed.

Any such approach is so far removed from the real needs of human beings that it is hardly worth serious consideration. What merits careful investigation is the factors which deprive individuals of the opportunity to marry if they wish to do so. There are clearly sociological reasons such as the inequality of numbers of men and women, but this is no longer a significant factor in Britain. There are the special home situations when a child, usually the daughter, is left with the responsibility of looking after ailing or elderly parents. There may be individual conflict for the woman between marriage and her professional life.

When all these and other minor sociological explanations have been exhausted, we are left with a small army of men and women who have not been able to marry in their twenties and early thirties for psychological reasons of which they are largely unaware. A few decades ago they would have accepted their predicament as an act of fate or, if they were believers, as the will of God, rationalised it in a satisfactory way and spent their single life richly and fully knowing that they had a significance in their own family milieu and in the community. Today, with the breakdown of the extended family structure and so many other changes, this solution is no longer easily tenable or satisfying.

One answer is to remain single and have a separate sexual life. Christianity cannot and must not accept this solution, not primarily on the grounds that pre-marital or extra-marital sex is evil, but because of the attack on human integrity that such a philosophy implies. Justice can never be done to human sexuality if the physical is isolated from a relationship of whole persons and this must remain the goal of human beings. Wholeness requires the presence of ongoing relationships in which the bonds of affection are served by physical sexuality in a process which allows the sustaining, growing and healing components to be present in the physical, emotional, social and spiritual encounter. If Christianity has run the risk of fragmenting human beings by devaluing the significance of physical sexuality in the past, there is an infinitely greater danger of fragmentation and loss of integrity when the body is isolated from the social, emotional and spiritual aspects of the whole person.

Other People and the Self

Instead, the specific contribution of Christianity must

be to focus attention on an increasing understanding of the reasons that prevent people who wish to marry from doing so, and to help them overcome the obstacles. The evidence suggests that these are overwhelmingly psychological. Such men and women are frequently sensitive, anxious people who find closeness overwhelmingly difficult. Deep in their personality are fears of being overwhelmed and trapped into childlike situations in the hands of others, and frequently they are imbued with a deep sense of mistrust and fear of persons of the opposite sex. Furthermore, even when they come to terms with these specific issues they have to overcome marked lack of self-esteem which means that they are unable to feel themselves as attractive, desirable or really having anything good in themselves which others want. They are often placed in an acutely painful situation where they desperately desire to feel wanted and appreciated and yet, as soon as someone offers them these feelings, withdraw in an acute panic. They cannot accept these tokens of being desirable because there is no part of their personality which has learned to feel at home with and to respond to such overtures.

This is a very common situation and leads to immense suffering, as hope is aroused only to be dashed repeatedly. It also causes some of the real tragedies in which the woman allows herself to be sufficiently involved sexually to become pregnant without either partner having the capacity to pursue the relationship any further. If an abortion is sought, the emotional and spiritual distress is enormous; if the pregnancy is not interrupted and a child is made to begin life without a father, then, however rationalised, an immense injustice is perpetrated on that child which needs and has the right to have both parents in the course of its formative years. Adoption, perhaps the most satisfactory solution for the child, can be excruciatingly painful for the mother.

The anxieties and suffering experienced by men and women in their middle thirties onwards who gradually realise that their youth is slipping by and they are no longer able to rationalise their single state, can be acute and prolonged. If under these circumstances they behave impulsively and irrationally, then they require unlimited compassion and constructive help.

Constructive help may be specialised psychological treatment which will allow them slowly to overcome their anxieties and self-rejection so that they can more easily form personal relationships. There are, of course, no short cuts to this nor any magical solutions. Nevertheless, psychotherapy has advanced immensely our capacity to negotiate these problems, even if the means available are still far from perfect.

Unfortunately the available help is indeed still extremely restricted. Here is an area in which Christianity should develop extensively if it is really going to meet the needs of such people. Even without expert treatment, such men and women have to be helped to realise their potential to the full. Often this means reassuring them about their personal gifts, so that they learn to use these effectively and negotiate the threat of being alone and isolated. Once their anxieties are diminished in this way, the Christian community should be in a position to confirm their significance and give them a valued place in its midst. Their acceptance of the single state through recognition of their unique personal value, rather than as an expression of despair, failure, resignation and hopelessness, must be the goal.

The Way of Celibacy

'But', Jesus said, 'it is not everyone who can accept what I have said, but only those to whom it is granted. There are eunuchs born that way from their mother's womb, there are eunuchs made so by men and there are eunuchs who have made themselves that way for the sake of the kingdom of heaven. Let anyone accept this who can.'[2]

What is granted? In the midst of an unprecedented consciousness of the significance of human sexuality there is a growing outcry that what is granted to those who pursue the single state is an unmitigated deprivation of their humanity. Such a view sounds little short of blasphemous to those concerned, who have followed and believed utterly in their dedication to God.

The traditional reasons for celibacy are well known. Based on the text just quoted and others, celibates are considered able to devote themselves more fully and wholeheartedly to God. Their presence in the world is a reminder of the mystery of Christ and his mission and an anticipation of the eschatological reality which affirms that in the resurrection there will be no marriage.

All this, clear and precise as it is, does not eliminate the inheritance of the past, which tended to compare marriage unfavourably with the single state and was undoubtedly related to a poor understanding of the value and significance of sexuality. Now that marriage has received in Vatican II a penetrating and unequivocal affirmation (even though the statement needs further development), it is inevitable that many feel doubtful about the significance of the single state.

What follows is the contribution of one married person who has no doubt about the significance of the single state dedicated to the service of God and considers it one of the precious jewels of the Christian tradition and particularly of the Catholic Church.

In order to reach this conclusion, it is important to eliminate any remaining doubts that celibacy may be an escape from the challenge of the world and of being fully human, and that it may deny the significance of sexuality. For those who have not entered the priesthood or religious life consciously or unconsciously because they are afraid to face life, or through other social or psychological rationalisations or because of fear or denial of their sexuality, the significance of this state is to be found in one word, *availability*,[3] modelled on Christ's availability to himself and to others.

The gospels portray vividly Christ's physical availability to his disciples, the crowds and the individuals who wanted to reach him. Again and again he goes out of his way to reach and be reached. This is a characteristic which has been preserved in the best tradition of Catholic priests and nuns. Even the monastic communities have demonstrated their availability for centuries to all those in need who have approached them. The absence of the physical availability of the enclosed orders needs, in our age, further consideration, but there can be no doubt about their spiritual availability to the rest of the community.

No one reading the gospels can have any doubts that Christ was available to all, independent of social class, race, belief or sex. The emphasis of this century on pulling down the social barriers which divide was anticipated by the Son of God whose love for human beings knew of no social boundaries. It is imperative that the single person, following in the footsteps of Christ, should be constantly clear about this evangelical counsel of perfection and alter course whenever the situation demands it. There can be no compromise over this, and the multiple examples of Christians who give testimony with their lives and work are some of the most precise statements of Christ's presence in the world today. Unhampered by obligations to the family, it is sometimes only the single person who can make this demonstration.

This subject is treated more extensively in an article called 'Human and Divine Love' in the September 1970 issue of *New Blackfriars*.[4] Essentially the points made there are that Christ possessed a high degree of empathy by means of which he could identify the inner world of others and respond accurately to their state. Furthermore, since he was able to accept himself completely he could combine these two characteristics of self-acceptance and empathy to reach the needs of others which he could feel emotionally and understand intellectually in their entirety. This response was unhampered by any need to reject, deny or condemn any part of himself, hence of others. He could reach others and help them to reach those parts of themselves which needed changing, growth and maturation, and his charismatic qualities must certainly have reflected this ability of reaching and being reached easily and completely. Although the evidence is extremely limited, it is hard to see how such total self-acceptance and availability could have been present without including full awareness of his sexuality.[5]

Christ offered his own and the Father's total non-judgemental, empathetic availability to his immediate world and through them to all humanity in the continuation of his Church. There can be no continuation of Christianity, of the total love of God for man, without evidence of it, and the single state dedicated to God is one precise manifestation of service through availability in the name of Christ.

VIII

The Power of Positive Love

THE SECOND VATICAN Council registered with unequivocal force the significance of the massive changes that have taken place in our age and the need for an appropriate response on the part of the Church. What an appropriate response should be has clearly been a matter of acute controversy in the field of sexuality and it could not be otherwise, for the changes in this sphere have been extreme and rapid and have impinged on Christianity in one of its most vulnerable areas. Under the circumstances no development is possible without marked controversy. The only really distressing factor is to be found when people of equal sincerity forget in the heat of the exchange that they all belong to the same Church, and resort to personal exchanges devoid of care and love.

It is not difficult to understand how these situations arise. Those who seek change feel at times betrayed by Mother Church when they adopt a particular stance, and the protagonists of traditional orientations feel equally betrayed and threatened when attitudes formerly considered unalterable are challenged fundamentally. Furthermore, since in the realm of sexuality and marriage much of the desired change owes its origins to the disciplines of psychology and sociology which have been basically foreign to the traditional categories of theological thought, there is the added mistrust and suspicion of having to integrate relatively new and untried ideas.

Those who care deeply about Christianity and the faith are bound to be aware of the inevitable pain this situation causes to many on both sides. As was stated in the first chapter in this book, the only justification for continuous exploration of a delicate and controversial area is the awareness that many sincere people feel that they need to repudiate their faith and seek fulfilment outside it if they are to do justice to their humanity. For too long they have been condemned and criticised for being disobedient, irresponsible and pleasure-seeking. These charges are occasionally right but, in the majority of cases, they are not. If the world appears to have abandoned Christ, we must make sure that the reason is not that the Church has abandoned the world because it has become too complex and difficult to understand and appreciate. It is the opinion of many, including myself, that in certain situations this is precisely what has happened. The most urgent task of today is for Christianity to give support to man's growing self-awareness, realising his potential, furthering the image of God reflected in him.

Others will certainly disagree with this view and sympathise with the words of St Paul to the Ephesians:

So be very careful about the sort of lives you lead, like intelligent and not like senseless people. This may be a wicked age, but your lives should redeem it.[1]

Before the arguments can proceed any further it is important that we should be clear what the differences of opinion are. And this is what this final article is devoted to.

The Goodness of Sexuality

The past has tended to see physical sexuality as something powerful, tending to be disruptive, at times uncontrollable and therefore dangerous. Christianity saved sexuality from the collective heresies that attacked the body and procreation but was not prepared to accord it any unique meaning or value of its own. Our age is trying to do just this and it is the contention of many Christians that this is correct and that the roots of this attitude are to be found in the Scriptures. In accepting this change certain precautions have to be taken.

First, Christianity must ensure that sexuality itself is rehabilitated and not wrongly used by those who seek an imaginary millenium of absolute freedom and become degenerate and licentious. Sexuality is a powerful force and its energy should be harnessed for man's good, not his destruction.

This good should respect the sexual integrity of the personality in its various stages of development and should be at the service of personal relationships. Here Christianity has a unique responsibility to society to clarify the character of truly authentic human relationships. It cannot do this, however, if its motives are suspect and if people feel that a lofty language is used to deprive them of their sexual potential and fulfilment.

Traditional Christianity is deeply suspicious that words like 'sexual fulfilment' are euphemisms for fornication, adultery and sheer hedonism. This, of course, can never be the case. Sexual fulfilment means sexual joy in the presence of relationships of integrity. So often, however, the dialogue ceases here because those who attack the new attitudes find it difficult to visualise what this development really means, and those who have experienced the sexual fulfilment and know it from personal experience feel that they can dismiss the warnings as prejudiced and irrelevant compared to the insights which they have acquired. Sadly, at this point they cease practising their faith, leave the Church and seek to influence it from outside. They must be free, of course, to choose this path but it is a solution tinged with despair.

If the changes advocated are right, then they must persuade by their relevance to authentic needs of men and women of this age.

One of the authentic changes of the age is its passionate insistence that the sexual should be faced openly. In this respect the Christian community has to meet a totally new situation from the recent past when so much of the subject was taboo. The emphasis was on silence, avoidance and facing the temptations by consciously distancing ourselves from the topic. Hence the anger and resentment that the subject has been widely advertised through the mass media. Here a choice lies before us. Either we attempt to continue to deal with it on a basis of ignorance and/or avoidance, or we make sexuality a central feature of Christian education for all children and adults, in home, school and parish.

By sexual education is meant the biology, psychology, sociology and theology of the subject and not just physical facts. These chapters have been written with the conviction that this is the only desirable course. Purity in the future will come from men and women who are not afraid to face sex, developing an internal security about it through which they can distinguish the authentic from the trivial, the distorted and the cheap which will be inescapably present. There are those who sincerely believe that this is an unrealistic idealism and that society is best safeguarded by keeping a vigilant censorship.

Much can be said for either side but, as a psychiatrist, I know that no censorship can ever exist as far as fantasy and imagination are concerned. The purity of heart that Our Lord was seeking can only come from an internal maturity that does not suppress or repress but discerns and differentiates openly and with confidence.

This does not mean to say that the infantile, poverty-stricken and appalling artistic quality of pornography and certain theatrical shows should not be rejected. It should be, on the basis of its utter inadequacy to do justice to the reality of authentic sex – beauty, joy, pathos, humour and conflict. And necessary care is needed to ensure that no one is subjected to any unwarranted invasion of their privacy.

This is all very well, some will say, but this lofty language does not face the simple issue that, if rules are relaxed, frail men and women are likely to pursue the line of least resistance and seek pleasure whenever and as often as they find it. Such critics will declare that only strict rules and discipline can safeguard man and that this is precisely what Christianity has given in the past, thus protecting the common good even if keeping the level of expectation low. They will warn that those who raise expectation and disregard the necessary discipline are really endangering the good of human beings who are frail and easily tempted, and back this view by quoting the figures of venereal disease, abortions and other undesirable consequences.

This is a serious charge too often ridiculed by those who are really concerned to attack authority, the establishment and any form of personal restriction. It has to be repeated that a genuine revaluation of sexuality does not aim at licence or chaos, nor at any reduction of personal discipline.

This criticism, nevertheless, misses the whole point at issue. Man as a free being is always able to misuse his gifts, and the risk must be taken because it is far more damaging to the Good News to deny the human potential for loving.

The insights from the disciplines of psychology and psychoanalysis are showing categorically that sex is a most powerful means of constructing, maintaining and reinforcing human bonds of affection and love. To deny these means is to dehumanise. While men and women are capable of adapting at various levels of dehumanisation, Christianity can never be true to its roots if it does not encourage the members of the Body of Christ to deepen their capacities to love their neighbour as themselves.

In the end sexuality serves love most forcefully and there can be no compromise with this insight. The risks must not be minimised, but nor must they be exaggerated. Too little attention is paid to the presence of intrinsic defence-mechanisms that human beings possess and exercise for their own care, protection and survival. It is necessary to educate for maturity from the earliest years of life and then to trust that maturity.

To achieve this we need extensive and deepening knowledge about the human personality and its functioning in the sphere of sex. I have advocated repeatedly[2] that one of the most urgent priorities in the Christian community is the establishment of centres in which basic research on sexuality and marriage will be carried out and the fruits of this knowledge made available to all those concerned with the care and service of the family and its members.

Christianity has poured out its resources on education in the past and, despite the criticism that is uttered in certain quarters about our schools, much is owed to the sacrifices and vision of those few. The time is now appropriate to extend this vision to a different area and concentrate on the characteristics of love in human relationships. One of the most important needs for advanced societies is to integrate and evaluate their rapidly emerging knowledge in the disciplines of biology, psychology, psychiatry and sociology so that man's integrity is safe-guarded, the much-used word 'love' clarified and its meaning deepened in personal relationships.

If Christianity safeguarded the truth about the basic goodness of the body in its first few centuries and repeatedly thereafter, it has now to proclaim unequivocally the joy and goodness of sexuality to an age that longs to experience this but is confused. The challenge facing Christianity today is to make a vital breakthrough which can inspire men and women with optimism about sexuality and with love for one another as an alternative to human exploitation and denigration. To do so, it has to devote a substantial amount of its resources to research on the meaning of love and communicate its findings to a world eager and hungry to receive but disconnected from the roots of the Good News which is the source of all love.

NOTES

THE CHURCH AND THE SEXUAL REVOLUTION

1. Mentor-Omega, 1967.
2. *Christian Freedom in a Permissive Society*. (SCM Press, 1970.)
3. SCM Press, 1966.
4. Philadelphia Westminster Press, 1966.
5. Rustum Roy and Della Roy. (George Allen and Unwin, 1969.)
6. A. Lunn and G. Lean. (London, Blandford Press, 1964.)
7. Collins, 1969.
8. Hosea 2: 19.
9. Exodus 20: 17.
10. Song of Songs 7: 2-5.
11. J. Blenkinsopp *Sexuality and the Christian Tradition*. (Sheed and Ward, 1970.)
12. Longmans, 1959.
13. J. Dominian. *Christian Marriage*, Chap. 2. (Darton, Longman and Todd, 1967.)

THE NATURE OF SEXUALITY

1. In Volume VII of the Standard Edition. Edited by James Strachey. (The Hogarth Press, London.)
2. *Ibid.*, p. 135.
3. I. Rosen. *The Pathology and Treatment of Sexual Deviation*. (Oxford Medical Publications, 1964.) Pp. 40-41.
4. Robert J. Stoller. *Sex and Gender*. (Hogarth Press, 1968.)
5. *Attachment and Loss*. (Hogarth Press, 1969.)
6. *Ibid.*, p. 230.

GROWING TOWARDS MARRIAGE

1. A. Comfort. *Sex in Society*. (Pelican, 1963.)
2. E. H. Erikson. *Identity*. (Faber, 1968.) P. 156.

3. The figure of 350,000 was reached by extrapolating the findings on a sample of 1,873 young people aged 15-19 from a random selection of seven areas in England and Wales.

SEXUALITY IN MARRIAGE

1. Ephesians 5: 31-32.
2. J. Dominian. *The Ampleforth Journal,* Vol. LXXXII, Part i, 1968.
3. J. Dominian. *The Tablet,* October 1969.
4. J. Marshall. *The Infertile Period.* (Darton, Longman and Todd, 1967.) Chap. II.
5. A. C. Kinsey, et al. *Sexual Behaviour in the Human Male.* (W. B. Sanders, 1934.) P. 234.
6. *Contributions to Psychoanalysis.* (Hogarth Press, 1950.)
7. Deuteronomy 22: 22.
8. Mark 10-19.
9. John 8: 1-11.

CHILDREN

1. *Marriage and Family in the Modern World in the Document of Vatican II.* (Geoffrey Chapman, 1966.)
2. W. Taylor. 'The Changing Pattern of Mortality in England and Wales.' *Infant Mortality. Brit. J. Soc. Med.* (1954.)
3. *The Registrar General's Statistical Review of England and Wales For the Year 1968.*
4. D. Warburton, C. F. Fraser. 'Spontaneous Abortion Risks in Man', *Human Genetics* XVI (1964).
5. J. Dominian. *Christian Marriage*; chapters 6 and 7. Darton, Longman and Todd—Libra books.

SEXUAL DEVIATIONS

1. D. J. West. *Homosexuality.* (Pelican.) P. 38.
2. Leading article in *BMJ,* 8 February 1969, 'Female Homosexuality'.
3. F. J. Kallman. *J. nerv. ment. dis.* 1952; 115, 283.
4. D. J. West. *Int. J. Soc. Psych.* 1959; 5, 85.
5. F. E. Kenyon. *J. Neurol, Neurosurgery, Psychiat.* 1968; 13, 487.
6. F. E. Kenyon. *Brit. J. Psychiat.* 1968; 114, 1337.

THE SINGLE STATE

1. *The Registrar General's Statistical Review of England and Wales for the year 1968.*
2. Matthew 19: 11-12.
3. J. Dominian. *The Available Priesthood in the Sacred Ministry.* Ed. G. R. Dunstan. (SPCK, 1970.)
4. J. Dominian. *New Blackfriars*, Vol. 51, September 1970.
5. 'Christ's Sexual Identity' will be the subject of a paper in a forthcoming Hedley Lecture.

THE POWER OF POSITIVE LOVE

1. Ephesians 5: 15-16.
2. See, e.g., 'To Serve the New Poor' (*Theology* LXX, October 1967); 'Modern Marriage Within the Church' (*The Tablet*, 11 October 1970).